Social Empowerment Learning Framework

High School Edition — Student Workbook

Created and written by Cedric A. Washington
Executive Director, NERD Youth Services, Inc.
Author | Educator | TEDx Speaker

TM

Table of Contents

Unit 1: SELF Conscience

TM

Unit 2: SELF Governing

Unit 3: Social Conscience

- Lesson 5: Accountability

- Lesson 6: Community Service and Giving Back

- Lesson 7: Building Your Legacy

Unit 4: Aspirations

- Lesson 1: What I Want to Be When I Grow Up

- Lesson 2: Career Day Panel Preparation and Event

- Lesson 3: Resume Workshop

- Lesson 4: Short Term Goals

- Lesson 5: Long Term Goals

- Lesson 6: Financial Literacy

- Lesson 7: Building Wealth and Generational Legacy

Unit 5: Good People Skills

- Lesson 1: Conflict Resolution

- Lesson 2: Group Cooperation

- Lesson 3: Friendship

- Lesson 4: Identifying Unhealthy Relationships

- Lesson 5: Self-Love

- Lesson 6: Communication Skills

- Lesson 7: Emotional Intelligence

Knowledge of SELF Curriculum — High School Student Workbook

© 2025 by Cedric A. Washington

Who Lives Like This?! Publishing LLC
www.nerdyouthservices.org

ISBN: 978-1-970680-10-2 (Paperback)

Cover design and interior layout by
Who Lives Like This?! Publishing LLC Design Team

Printed in the United States of America

First Edition — 2025

About the Author

Cedric A. Washington is a master educator, speaker, author, former college basketball player, and the Executive Director of NERD Youth Services, Inc. A native of Gary, Indiana. Over two decades of experience in education, mentoring, and community leadership have fueled his commitment to building culturally responsive, empowering programs for African American youth. As the visionary behind the Knowledge of SELF (Social Empowerment Learning Framework) curriculum, Cedric blends historical awareness, emotional intelligence, leadership training, and personal reflection to cultivate greatness in every student he reaches. His work has been celebrated nationally at education conferences, faith institutions, and youth leadership summits. Cedric's mission is simple but powerful: To equip young people with the self-knowledge, discipline, and purpose they need to transform themselves — and the world.

Daily Affirmations

I AM a trailblazer. I AM destined to succeed. Speak it. Believe it. Do it. – Cedric A. Washington

- I am enough, just as I am.
- My history is powerful, my future is greater.
- I am not what the world calls me—I am who God created me to be.
- I will lead with love, courage, and clarity.
- My skin, my hair, my mind—divinely designed.
- I rise above every label and lie.
- Greatness is not ahead of me; it's within me.
- I walk in wisdom and purpose.
- I am part of a legacy of excellence.
- I build, I uplift, I transform.

Pre-Reflection Survey

Before starting the Knowledge of SELF curriculum, please answer honestly:

1. What do you currently know about your cultural identity?

2. How confident are you in making positive decisions for your future? (1–5)

3. What does success mean to you?

4. Have you ever felt misunderstood in school or in life? Explain.

5. What do you hope to gain from this experience?

TM

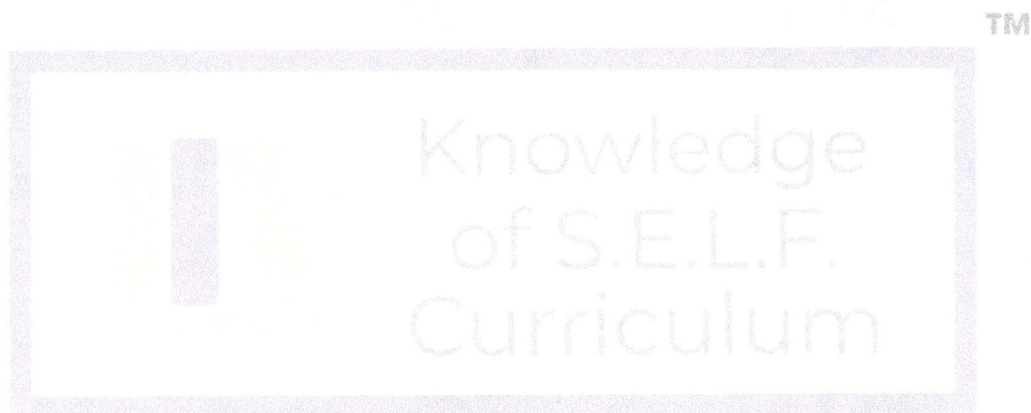

Knowledge of SELF (Social Empowerment Learning Framework)

High School Edition — Student Workbook ™

Unit One: SELF Conscience

Lesson 1: Am I a Color? (Part 1)

Objective:
Students will critically explore identity, history, and ethnicity beyond societal labels.

Do Now:
Do you recognize yourself as an African American? If yes, what does that mean to you?

_____

_____

_____

_____

_____

_____

_____

_____

Reflection:
Discuss the different labels historically placed on African Americans: Negro, Colored, Black, African American, Afro American.
How do these terms relate to ethnicity vs. nationality?

_____

_____

_____

_____

_____

_____

_____

_____

Activity:
- Read definitions: Ethnicity and Nationality.
- Discuss: Which term truly defines your identity?
- Reflect on Africa as a continent with 54 countries—where do African Americans trace their roots?

Critical Thinking Questions:

1. Can you have true self-awareness without knowledge of self?

_____

_____

_____

_____

_____

_____

_____

_____

_____

_____

2. Why is it important to question the historical narratives taught to us?

_____

_____

_____

_____

_____

_____

_____

_____

_____

_____

Biblical Reference Exploration:
- Genesis Chapters 6–10
- Genesis 42:6–8, 23
- Exodus 2:19
- Deuteronomy 28
- Revelation 1:14–15

Journal Prompt:
What are your thoughts right now about the identity of the so-called "African American"?
[Write two full paragraphs.]

Lesson 2: Am I a Color? (Part 2)

Objective:
Students will deepen their understanding of historical disconnection and reclaim true identity.

Do Now:
What is the purpose of going to church?
What is the purpose of going to school?
List two similarities between church and school.

_____
_____
_____
_____
_____
_____
_____
_____
_____
_____

Discussion:
- Explore the Bible as a historical text — why is pre-slavery history rarely taught?
- Open dialogue on separation of church and state.

Critical Thinking Questions:
1. If the Bible contains historical information, why isn't it taught in history classes?

_____
_____
_____
_____
_____
_____
_____

2. Why does the teaching of African American history often begin with slavery?

_____
_____
_____
_____
_____
_____

Activity:
- View Deuteronomy 28 ("The Curses")
- Explore the Trans-Atlantic Slave Trade history
- Discuss the stripping of language, culture, religion from enslaved Africans.

Journal Prompt:
Reflect on why true historical knowledge has been hidden and what it means for reclaiming your power.
[Write two full paragraphs.]

Lesson 3: Love Yourself (The Skin You're In)

Objective:

Students will embrace their natural beauty and critically analyze societal definitions of race and color.

Do Now:

Take a deep dive into the definitions of the word 'black' and 'white'. What emotions come up when you hear the words "Black" or "White" to describe people?

_____
_____
_____
_____
_____
_____
_____
_____

Mini-Lesson:

- Define Melanin: Its role, beauty, and protection properties.
- Explore: Melanin is made of 6 protons, 6 neutrons, and 6 electrons — the true meaning behind "666" (often misrepresented).

Activity:
- Match your skin tone on the Skin Tone Chart.
- Discuss the power of words: Define "Black" and "White" from Merriam-Webster.
- Analyze why "Black" is described negatively and "White" positively in society.

"I don't want to be in the sun too long because I don't want to get black." How many times have we either heard or said this comment? The very thing that we don't want to get is the sole source of our dominance, melanin. ***Melanin is made up of 6 protons, 6 neutrons, and 6 electrons, 666.*** When the numbers 666 are often mentioned it's referred by mainstream media as the mark of the beast.

However, when you gain knowledge of SELF, one begins to learn that the so called African American or black people aren't even the color that they sing loud and proud **about**. Look at the Skin Tone Chart and match your skin complexion with the shades of brown   on the Skin Tone Chart.

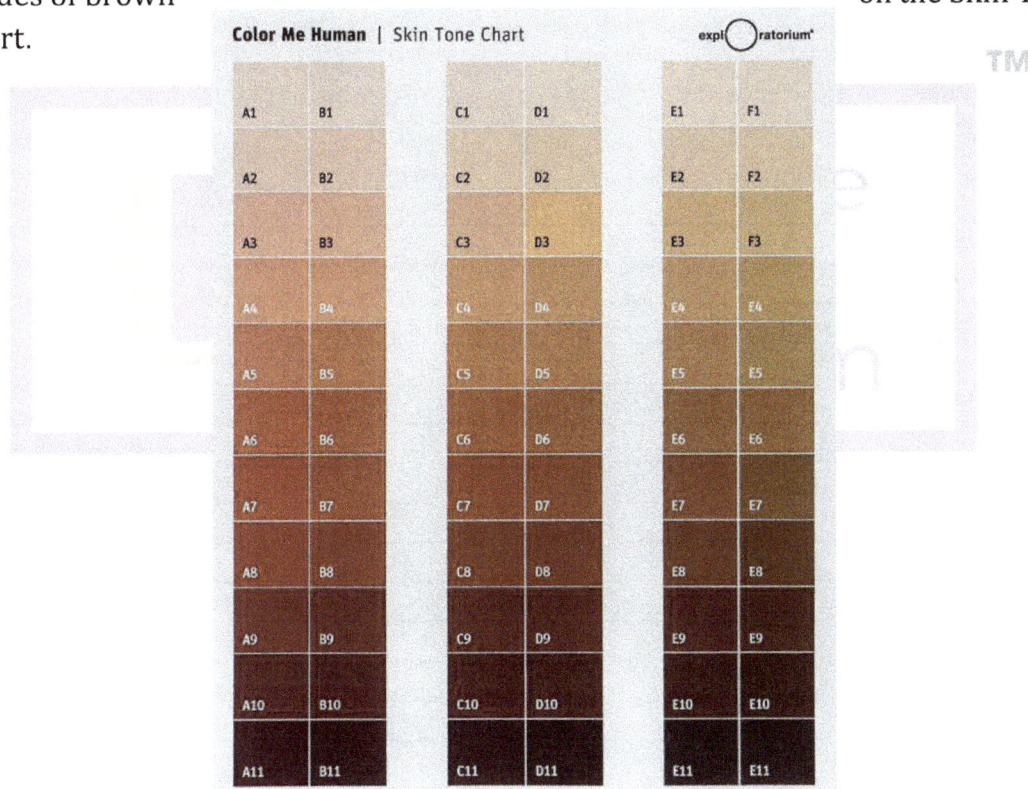

Color Me Human | Skin Tone Chart   expl◯ratorium®

TM

A1	B1	C1	D1	E1	F1
A2	B2	C2	D2	E2	F2
A3	B3	C3	D3	E3	F3
A4	B4	C4	D4	E4	E4
A5	B5	C5	D5	E5	E5
A6	B6	C6	D6	E6	E6
A7	B7	C7	D7	E7	E7
A8	B8	C8	D8	E8	E8
A9	B9	C9	D9	E9	E9
A10	B10	C10	D10	E10	E10
A11	B11	C11	D11	E11	E11

Critical Thinking Questions:
1. How does redefining yourself impact how you navigate the world?

_____
_____
_____
_____
_____

2. Why is knowledge of your true beauty revolutionary?

_____

_____

_____

_____

_____

_____

_____

_____

_____

_____

_____

_____

Journal Prompt:
After today's lesson, how do you view your skin, your melanin, and your identity differently?
[Write two full paragraphs.]

_____

_____

_____

_____

_____

_____

_____

_____

_____

_____

_____

_____

_____

_____

_____

_____

Lesson 4: Attributes/Characteristics of SELF

Objective:
Students will reflect on and define their personal attributes, strengths, and areas for growth.

Do Now:
What are three qualities you are most proud of about yourself?

_____
_____
_____
_____
_____
_____
_____
_____

Mini-Lesson:
- Self-conscience means understanding your inner traits, not just your experiences.
- True empowerment comes from reflection, not reaction.

Activity:
Self-Inventory Exercise:
- List your five greatest strengths.
- List your two biggest weaknesses.
- Name three traits you admire in others.

Critical Thinking Questions:
1. Why is self-awareness important for growth and leadership?

_____
_____
_____
_____
_____
_____
_____
_____
_____
_____

2. How does knowing your strengths and weaknesses shape your future choices?

_____
_____
_____
_____
_____
_____
_____
_____
_____
_____

Journal Prompt:
Who are you becoming — and why is it important to know the answer?
[Write two full paragraphs.]

_____
_____
_____
_____
_____
_____
_____
_____
_____
_____
_____
_____
_____
_____
_____
_____
_____
_____

Lesson 5: Ethics

Objective:
Students will explore their personal values and understand how ethics guide decision-making.

Do Now:
List three things you believe are most important in life.

_____
_____
_____
_____
_____
_____
_____
_____

Mini-Lesson:
- Ethics are the compass guiding you when no one is watching.
- Living by principles builds legacy.

Activity:
Personal Values Reflection:
- Write 10 things that are important to you.
- Narrow it down to your top 3 values.

Critical Thinking Questions:
1. How do your values impact the decisions you make every day?

_____
_____
_____
_____
_____
_____
_____
_____

2. Why is living ethically important for leadership and respect?

_____
_____
_____
_____
_____
_____
_____
_____
_____

Journal Prompt:

Describe a moment when you chose to do the right thing, even when it was hard.
[Write two full paragraphs.]

_____
_____
_____
_____
_____
_____
_____
_____
_____
_____
_____
_____
_____
_____
_____
_____
_____
_____
_____
_____

Lesson 6: Image

Objective:
Students will analyze the difference between public image and private authenticity.

Do Now:
Do you ever feel pressured to present a certain image to others? Explain.

_____
_____
_____
_____
_____
_____
_____

Mini-Lesson:
- Public image is how others see you.
- Private self is who you are when no one is watching.

Activity:
Image Mapping:
- Create two lists: "Public Me" and "Private Me."
- Compare and reflect on the differences.

Critical Thinking Questions:
1. How can living authentically improve your confidence and peace?

_____
_____
_____
_____
_____
_____
_____
_____
_____
_____

2. Why is it dangerous to build a life around pleasing others?

_____
_____
_____
_____
_____
_____
_____
_____

Journal Prompt:
How do you want to be remembered when your name is mentioned years from now?
[Write two full paragraphs.]

_____
_____
_____
_____
_____
_____
_____
_____
_____
_____
_____
_____
_____
_____
_____
_____
_____
_____
_____
_____
_____

Lesson 7: Achievements

Objective:
Students will celebrate their past achievements and set goals for future impact.

Do Now:
Name one thing you've accomplished that you are truly proud of.

_____
_____
_____
_____
_____
_____
_____
_____
_____

Mini-Lesson:
- Achievements are evidence that hard work and faith produce fruit.
- Big or small, every win matters.

Activity:
Achievement Reflection:
- List three achievements you are most proud of.
- Write one achievement you are aiming to accomplish in the next year.

Critical Thinking Questions:
1. How does reflecting on your achievements build confidence for new challenges?

_____
_____
_____
_____
_____
_____
_____
_____
_____
_____

2. Why is it important to celebrate your own growth instead of waiting for outside approval?

_____

_____

_____

_____

_____

_____

_____

Journal Prompt:

What legacy do you want your achievements to create?

[Write two full paragraphs.]

_____

_____

_____

_____

_____

_____

_____

_____

_____

_____

_____

_____

_____

_____

_____

_____

_____

_____

_____

_____

_____

Knowledge of SELF (Social Empowerment Learning Framework)

High School Edition — Student Workbook ™

Unit Two: SELF Governing

Lesson 1: Health and Nutrition

Objective:
Students will understand how physical health and nutrition impact personal power, mental focus, and leadership.

Do Now:
What is one healthy habit you already practice? How has it helped you?

_____
_____
_____
_____
_____
_____
_____
_____
_____

Mini-Lesson:
- Your body is your first home — what you feed it fuels your mind and spirit.
- Good health = Greater energy for purpose.

Activity:
Health Awareness Mapping:
- List 3 healthy habits you already do.
- List 3 habits you want to improve.
- Discuss how foods like sea moss, fruits, water, and greens nourish your power.

Critical Thinking Questions:
1. Why is treating your body well an act of self-respect?

_____
_____
_____
_____
_____
_____
_____
_____
_____
_____

2. How can improving your nutrition sharpen your focus, discipline, and leadership?

_____

_____

_____

_____

_____

_____

_____

_____

Journal Prompt:
What is one change you will commit to for better health starting today?
[Write two full paragraphs.]

_____

_____

_____

_____

_____

_____

_____

_____

_____

_____

_____

_____

_____

_____

_____

_____

_____

_____

_____

_____

_____

_____

Lesson 2: The Importance of FOCUS

Objective:
Students will learn the F.O.C.U.S. method to move from dreams to disciplined action.

Do Now:
Describe a time you lost focus. What was the consequence?

_____
_____
_____
_____
_____
_____
_____
_____

Mini-Lesson:
- F.O.C.U.S. = Fallback, Opportunities, Cultivate, Understanding, Succeed.
- Focus requires sacrifice, vision, discipline, and understanding not everyone will understand.

Activity:
F.O.C.U.S. Breakdown:
- Fallback: Step back from distractions.
- Opportunities: Align with growth-minded people and places.
- Cultivate: Practice, fail, adjust, and sharpen skills.
- Understanding: Master that not everyone will understand your mission.
- Succeed: Celebrate small victories as stepping stones.

Critical Thinking Questions:
1. How does each step of the F.O.C.U.S. model build unstoppable discipline?

_____
_____
_____
_____
_____
_____
_____
_____
_____
_____

2. Why must you sometimes walk alone on the path to greatness?

_____

_____

_____

_____

_____

_____

_____

_____

Journal Prompt:

What dream requires you to F.O.C.U.S. harder starting today?

[Write two full paragraphs.]

_____

_____

_____

_____

_____

_____

_____

_____

_____

_____

_____

_____

_____

_____

_____

_____

_____

Special Highlight: Watch Cedric A. Washington's TED Talk on The Importance of Focus for inspiration!

Lesson 3: Role Modeling

Objective:
Students will understand the power of becoming role models through action, not words.

Do Now:
Who is one person you admire as a role model? Why?

_____
_____
_____
_____
_____
_____
_____
_____
_____
_____

Mini-Lesson:
- Leadership is visible — you are someone's example even if you don't realize it.
- Role modeling is not perfection; it's consistent effort.

Activity:
Role Model Reflection:
- List the traits you admire in your role models.
- List traits you are building to be a role model to others.

Critical Thinking Questions:
1. What responsibilities come with being a role model?

_____
_____
_____
_____
_____
_____
_____
_____
_____
_____
_____
_____

2. How does being a role model push you to elevate your own life?

_____

_____

_____

_____

_____

_____

_____

Journal Prompt:
What legacy do you want your leadership and example to leave?
[Write two full paragraphs.]

_____

_____

_____

_____

_____

_____

_____

_____

_____

_____

_____

_____

_____

_____

_____

_____

_____

_____

_____

Lesson 4: Hygiene

Objective:
Students will understand the importance of self-care, hygiene, and personal presentation as a reflection of self-respect.

Do Now:
How does personal hygiene affect how you feel about yourself each day?

_____
_____
_____
_____
_____
_____
_____
_____
_____

Mini-Lesson:
- Cleanliness is a form of self-love.
- Your hygiene is the first statement you make before you ever speak.

Activity:
Self-Care Plan:
- List 5 daily hygiene habits you practice.
- Create a self-care checklist for your morning and evening routine.

Critical Thinking Questions:
1. How does personal care impact your confidence and opportunities?

_____
_____
_____
_____
_____
_____
_____
_____
_____
_____

2. Why is hygiene deeper than looks — it's about honoring your temple?

_____

_____

_____

_____

_____

_____

_____

Journal Prompt:
What habits will you commit to for mastering personal excellence?
[Write two full paragraphs.]

_____

_____

_____

_____

_____

_____

_____

_____

_____

_____

_____

_____

_____

_____

_____

_____

_____

_____

_____

_____

Lesson 5: Emotional Maturity

Objective:
Students will explore what it means to be emotionally mature and how it impacts leadership, relationships, and destiny.

Do Now:
Describe a time when you had to control your emotions for a better outcome.

_____
_____
_____
_____
_____
_____
_____
_____
_____
_____

Mini-Lesson:
- Emotional maturity is handling emotions with wisdom, not impulse.
- Leaders are respected not for being emotional, but for being emotionally wise.

Activity:
Emotional Wisdom Reflection:
- Identify 3 triggers that challenge your emotional control.
- Write strategies to manage them better.

Critical Thinking Questions:
1. How does emotional maturity give you power over situations?

_____
_____
_____
_____
_____
_____
_____
_____
_____
_____

2. Why is emotional self-control crucial for building trust and leadership?

_____

_____

_____

_____

_____

_____

_____

_____

Journal Prompt:
How will mastering your emotions transform your life?
[Write two full paragraphs.]

_____

_____

_____

_____

_____

_____

_____

_____

_____

_____

_____

_____

_____

_____

_____

_____

_____

_____

_____

_____

_____

Lesson 6: Puberty

Objective:
Students will learn how to navigate the physical, emotional, and psychological changes of puberty with understanding and empowerment.

Do Now:
What's one thing you wish adults would have explained better about growing up?

_____
_____
_____
_____
_____
_____
_____
_____
_____

Mini-Lesson:
- Puberty brings physical, mental, and emotional shifts — it's normal, but confusing.
- Knowing your body helps you control your mind and build confidence.

Activity:
Puberty Myth vs. Fact:
- Discuss and debunk common myths about puberty.
- Share tips for self-care, mental health, and emotional resilience.

Critical Thinking Questions:
1. Why is it important to normalize conversations about body changes?

_____
_____
_____
_____
_____
_____
_____
_____
_____
_____

2. How can knowledge and preparation reduce fear about growing up?

_____
_____
_____
_____
_____
_____
_____
_____

Journal Prompt:
What is one thing you will embrace or prepare for better as you continue to mature?
[Write two full paragraphs.]

_____
_____
_____
_____
_____
_____
_____
_____
_____
_____
_____
_____
_____
_____
_____
_____
_____
_____
_____
_____
_____
_____
_____

Lesson 7: Peer Pressure

Objective:
Students will learn how to identify peer pressure and develop strategies to stay true to their values.

Do Now:
Describe a time when you felt pressure from peers. How did you handle it?

_____
_____
_____
_____
_____
_____
_____
_____

Mini-Lesson:
- Pressure is real but so is power.
- Strength comes from setting boundaries and staying focused.

Activity:
Peer Pressure Role Play:
- Students act out different peer pressure scenarios and practice strong responses.

Critical Thinking Questions:
1. Why is staying true to yourself sometimes harder than going along?

_____
_____
_____
_____
_____
_____
_____
_____
_____
_____
_____
_____

2. How does resisting peer pressure shape your leadership and self-trust?

_____

_____

_____

_____

_____

_____

_____

_____

Journal Prompt:
What will you do differently the next time you face peer pressure?
[Write two full paragraphs.]

_____

_____

_____

_____

_____

_____

_____

_____

_____

_____

_____

_____

_____

_____

_____

_____

_____

_____

_____

_____

Knowledge of SELF (Social Empowerment Learning Framework)

High School Edition — Student Workbook ™

Unit Three: Social Conscience

Lesson 1: How to Be Effective in Your Community

Objective:
Students will understand how their leadership and service can create positive change in their communities.

Do Now:
What is one issue you would change in your community if you had the power?

_____
_____
_____
_____
_____
_____
_____

Mini-Lesson:
- Change doesn't come from complaining — it comes from commitment.
- True leadership starts locally, not nationally.

Activity:
Community Impact Mapping:
- List one major challenge in your community.
- Brainstorm three realistic actions you could take to start solving it.

Critical Thinking Questions:
1. How does solving problems at home impact the entire world?

_____
_____
_____
_____
_____
_____
_____
_____
_____
_____
_____
_____
_____
_____
_____
_____

2. Why is starting small sometimes more powerful than aiming big too soon?

_____
_____
_____
_____
_____
_____
_____
_____

Journal Prompt:
What community cause will you commit to standing for, starting now?
[Write two full paragraphs.]

_____
_____
_____
_____
_____
_____
_____
_____
_____
_____
_____
_____
_____
_____
_____
_____
_____
_____
_____
_____
_____
_____

Lesson 2: African American Leaders

Objective:
Students will explore the power of leadership within African American history and its relevance to their own potential.

Do Now:
Name one African American leader you admire. Why?

_____
_____
_____
_____
_____
_____
_____

Mini-Lesson:
- Our history is filled with warriors, builders, healers, and visionaries.
- Leadership is a responsibility you inherit when you know who you are.

Activity:
Leadership Reflection:
- Research and summarize the impact of one African American leader.
- Identify three traits you can model in your own life.

Critical Thinking Questions:
1. How does learning about past leaders strengthen your purpose today?

_____
_____
_____
_____
_____
_____
_____
_____

2. Why is it important to add your voice and legacy to our history?

_____

_____

_____

_____

_____

_____

_____

_____

Journal Prompt:

What kind of leader will you be for the next generation?

[Write two full paragraphs.]

_____

_____

_____

_____

_____

_____

_____

_____

_____

_____

_____

_____

_____

_____

_____

_____

_____

_____

_____

_____

_____

Lesson 3: Hip Hop: The Culture

Objective:
Students will analyze Hip Hop as a cultural force, both positive and challenging, and reclaim its power for empowerment.

Do Now:
What song or artist has influenced your mindset the most?

_____

_____

_____

_____

_____

_____

_____

_____

_____

Mini-Lesson:
- Hip Hop was born out of struggle, storytelling, and resilience.
- It can uplift, educate, or destroy — depending on how it's used.

Activity:
Culture Check:
- List three positive messages you hear in Hip Hop.
- List three negative messages you hear.
- Discuss how culture can be reclaimed for empowerment.

Critical Thinking Questions:
1. How can Hip Hop be a weapon for healing rather than harm?

_____

_____

_____

_____

_____

_____

_____

_____

2. Why must we guard what we consume and create?

_____
_____
_____
_____
_____
_____
_____
_____

Journal Prompt:
If you could create a Hip Hop anthem about your life, what would it say?
[Write two full paragraphs.]

_____
_____
_____
_____
_____
_____
_____
_____
_____
_____
_____
_____
_____
_____
_____
_____
_____
_____
_____
_____
_____
_____

Lesson 4: Family Dynamics

Objective:
Students will explore how family structures, values, and experiences shape their identity and leadership.

Do Now:
What is one positive value or lesson you've learned from your family?

_____
_____
_____
_____
_____
_____
_____
_____
_____
_____
_____
_____

Mini-Lesson:
- Family can build or break confidence — recognize your foundation, but choose your future.
- Healing and understanding your roots help you grow strong branches.

Activity:
Family Reflection:
- Create a "Family Tree of Strengths" highlighting values, sacrifices, and lessons passed down.

Critical Thinking Questions:
1. How does your family history affect the way you view yourself and the world?

_____
_____
_____
_____
_____
_____
_____
_____
_____
_____

2. Why is it important to honor your roots while building your own path?

_____

_____

_____

_____

_____

_____

_____

_____

Journal Prompt:
How will you build a future legacy stronger than your past?
[Write two full paragraphs.]

_____

_____

_____

_____

_____

_____

_____

_____

_____

_____

_____

_____

_____

_____

_____

_____

_____

_____

_____

_____

_____

Lesson 5: Accountability

Objective:
Students will understand accountability as the foundation of self-respect, leadership, and success.

Do Now:
Describe a time when taking responsibility helped you grow.

_____
_____
_____
_____
_____
_____
_____
_____

Mini-Lesson:
- Excuses are easy; accountability is excellence.
- Growth begins the moment you stop blaming and start owning.

Activity:
Accountability Map:
- Write three areas of your life where you will take stronger ownership.
- Create an "Accountability Partner Plan" — list someone who can help you stay on track.

Critical Thinking Questions:
1. How does accountability make your dreams more real?

_____
_____
_____
_____
_____
_____
_____
_____
_____
_____

2. Why is blaming others a barrier to becoming your best self?

_____
_____
_____
_____
_____
_____
_____
_____

Journal Prompt:
What area of your life are you ready to take full ownership of starting today?
[Write two full paragraphs.]

_____
_____
_____
_____
_____
_____
_____
_____
_____
_____
_____
_____
_____
_____
_____
_____
_____
_____
_____
_____
_____
_____
_____
_____

Lesson 6: Community Service and Giving Back

Objective:
Students will learn how giving back to their community strengthens their leadership and legacy.

Do Now:
Name one way someone helped you when they didn't have to. How did it impact you?

_____

_____

_____

_____

_____

_____

_____

Mini-Lesson:
- Service isn't charity — it's responsibility.
- Giving back multiplies blessings for both the giver and the receiver.

Activity:
Service Planning:
- Brainstorm three service projects you could lead in your community.

Critical Thinking Questions:
1. How does serving others build your leadership?

_____

_____

_____

_____

_____

_____

_____

_____

_____

2. Why is giving back one of the most powerful ways to heal a community?

_____
_____
_____
_____
_____
_____
_____
_____

Journal Prompt:
What service project will you commit to leading or participating in within the next year?
[Write two full paragraphs.]

_____
_____
_____
_____
_____
_____
_____
_____
_____
_____
_____
_____
_____
_____
_____
_____
_____
_____
_____

Lesson 7: Building Your Legacy

Objective:
Students will define what legacy means to them and begin crafting a personal vision for impact beyond their lifetime.

Do Now:
What do you want people to say about you 50 years from now?

_____

_____

_____

_____

_____

_____

_____

Mini-Lesson:
- Legacy isn't built someday — it's built daily.
- Every decision today shapes the world you leave behind.

Activity:
Legacy Blueprint:
- Write your "Legacy Mission Statement" — how you want to impact your family, community, and world.

Critical Thinking Questions:
1. Why is legacy more important than momentary success?

_____

_____

_____

_____

_____

_____

_____

_____

_____

_____

2. What daily habits are you willing to build to leave a legacy that matters?

_____
_____
_____
_____
_____
_____
_____
_____

Journal Prompt:
Describe the world you dream of building — and your role in bringing it to life.
[Write two full paragraphs.]

_____
_____
_____
_____
_____
_____
_____
_____
_____
_____
_____
_____
_____
_____
_____
_____
_____
_____
_____
_____
_____

Knowledge of SELF (Social Empowerment Learning Framework)

High School Edition — Student Workbook

Unit Four: Aspirations

Lesson 1: What I Want to Be When I Grow Up

Objective:
Students will visualize and define their future career and life goals, connecting purpose to passion.

Do Now:
If you could do any job in the world and succeed at it, what would it be?

_____
_____
_____
_____
_____
_____
_____
_____
_____
_____
_

Mini-Lesson:
- Dream boldly, but plan wisely.
- Your gift makes room for you, but discipline keeps you there.

Activity:
Dream Career Blueprint:
- Write down your dream career.
- List 3 steps you can take in the next 12 months to move toward it.

Critical Thinking Questions:
1. Why is it important to dream bigger than your circumstances?

_____
_____
_____
_____
_____
_____
_____
_____
_____
_____

2. How does purpose give your dreams fuel to survive challenges?

_____

_____

_____

_____

_____

_____

_____

_____

Journal Prompt:

Describe the future you want and what you're willing to sacrifice to create it.

[Write two full paragraphs.]

_____

_____

_____

_____

_____

_____

_____

_____

_____

_____

_____

_____

_____

_____

_____

_____

_____

_____

_____

_____

_____

_____

_____

_____

_____

Lesson 2: Career Day Panel Preparation and Event

Objective:
Students will prepare thoughtful questions and actively engage with career professionals to expand their knowledge and networks.

Do Now:
What is one career field you want to learn more about?

_____

_____

_____

_____

_____

_____

_____

_____

_____

Mini-Lesson:
- Exposure breeds expansion — meeting real professionals makes dreams feel reachable.
- Prepare questions that dig deep, not surface-level.

Activity:
Career Day Prep:
- Draft 5 powerful questions to ask panelists (e.g., What challenges did you face? What advice would you give your younger self?).

Critical Thinking Questions:
1. Why is it important to network with people already where you want to go?

_____

_____

_____

_____

_____

_____

_____

_____

_____

2. How can asking good questions open doors to opportunities?

_____
_____
_____
_____
_____
_____
_____
_____

Journal Prompt:

After Career Day, reflect: What is one lesson or piece of advice you will carry with you? [Write two full paragraphs.]

_____
_____
_____
_____
_____
_____
_____
_____
_____
_____
_____
_____
_____
_____
_____
_____
_____
_____
_____
_____

Lesson 3: Resume Workshop

Objective:
Students will build their first professional resume and understand the power of presenting their skills confidently.

Do Now:
List 3 skills, activities, or jobs you've already done that show your abilities.

_____
_____
_____
_____
_____
_____
_____
_____
_____

Mini-Lesson:
- A resume is your personal commercial.
- It's about showing who you are and what you bring to the table.

Activity:
Resume Building:
- Using a sample template, students draft their first resume highlighting skills, experience, leadership, and goals.

Critical Thinking Questions:
1. How can a strong resume build your confidence before even stepping into an interview?

_____
_____
_____
_____
_____
_____
_____
_____
_____
_____

2. Why is it important to continuously update your resume as you grow?

_____
_____
_____
_____
_____
_____
_____
_____

Journal Prompt:
What experiences or achievements will you work toward to make your resume even stronger this year?
[Write two full paragraphs.]

_____
_____
_____
_____
_____
_____
_____
_____
_____
_____
_____
_____
_____
_____
_____
_____
_____
_____
_____
_____

Lesson 4: Short Term Goals

Objective:
Students will define achievable short-term goals and build the habits necessary for consistent progress.

Do Now:
What is one thing you could accomplish within the next 30 days?

_____
_____
_____
_____
_____
_____
_____
_____
_____

Mini-Lesson:
- Big dreams require small wins.
- Short-term goals build momentum toward your long-term destiny.

Activity:
Short-Term Goal Setting:
- Write down one academic, one personal, and one career goal for the next 30–90 days.
- Identify one daily habit that will help achieve each goal.

Critical Thinking Questions:
1. Why are short-term goals essential to keeping hope and progress alive?

_____
_____
_____
_____
_____
_____
_____
_____
_____

2. How does achieving small goals shift your mindset and confidence?

_____

_____

_____

_____

_____

_____

_____

_____

Journal Prompt:
What short-term win will you celebrate in the next 30 days?
[Write two full paragraphs.]

_____

_____

_____

_____

_____

_____

_____

_____

_____

_____

_____

_____

_____

_____

_____

_____

_____

_____

_____

_____

Lesson 5: Long Term Goals

Objective:
Students will envision and create a blueprint for long-term success by planning years ahead.

Do Now:
Imagine your life 10 years from now — where are you? What are you doing?

_____
_____
_____
_____
_____
_____
_____
_____
_____

Mini-Lesson:
- Long-term goals give your life a mission.
- Without vision, you settle for survival instead of striving.

Activity:
Long-Term Dream Map:
- Write down your 5-year, 10-year, and 20-year visions for your life in career, health, finances, and impact.

Critical Thinking Questions:
1. Why is it important to plan not just for next year, but for the next decade?

_____
_____
_____
_____
_____
_____
_____
_____
_____
_____
_____

2. How does your vision influence your daily decisions today?

_____
_____
_____
_____
_____
_____
_____
_____

Journal Prompt:
What would you tell your future self 10 years from now?
[Write two full paragraphs.]

_____
_____
_____
_____
_____
_____
_____
_____
_____
_____
_____
_____
_____
_____
_____
_____
_____
_____
_____
_____
_____
_____
_____

Lesson 6: Financial Literacy

Objective:
Students will learn the basics of financial literacy including saving, budgeting, and investing for long-term wealth.

Do Now:
What is one thing you wish schools taught more about money?

_____
_____
_____
_____
_____
_____
_____
_____
_____
_____

Mini-Lesson:
- Wealth is not just about earning — it's about managing.
- Financial knowledge = financial freedom.

Activity:
Money Power Moves:
- Create a basic budget: Income vs. Expenses.
- Identify two money habits to build wealth (e.g., save 20%, invest early).

Critical Thinking Questions:
1. Why is mastering money a form of mastering your freedom?

_____
_____
_____
_____
_____
_____
_____
_____
_____

2. How does financial ignorance trap people in cycles of struggle?

_____

_____

_____

_____

_____

_____

_____

_____

Journal Prompt:
What is one money move you will commit to this year?
[Write two full paragraphs.]

_____

_____

_____

_____

_____

_____

_____

_____

_____

_____

_____

_____

_____

_____

_____

_____

_____

_____

_____

_____

_____

_____

Lesson 7: Building Wealth and Generational Legacy

Objective:
Students will learn the importance of building wealth not just for themselves but for future generations.

Do Now:
What does "generational wealth" mean to you?

_____

_____

_____

_____

_____

_____

_____

_____

_____

Mini-Lesson:
- Wealth is not about flash — it's about freedom, security, and legacy.
- You are the seed planter for the next century of your family tree.

Activity:
Legacy Wealth Plan:
- Write down 3 strategies you will use to build and protect generational wealth.

Critical Thinking Questions:
1. How does building wealth shift your family's future forever?

_____

_____

_____

_____

_____

_____

_____

_____

_____

2. Why must we think in terms of "we" (future family) instead of only "me"?

_____

_____

_____

_____

_____

_____

_____

_____

Journal Prompt:

What kind of world do you want your grandchildren to inherit — and how will you start building it today?

[Write two full paragraphs.]

_____

_____

_____

_____

_____

_____

_____

_____

_____

_____

_____

_____

_____

_____

_____

_____

_____

_____

_____

_____

Knowledge of SELF (Social Empowerment Learning Framework)™

High School Edition — Student Workbook

Unit Five: Good People Skills

Lesson 1: Conflict Resolution

Objective:
Students will learn strategies to resolve conflicts peacefully and protect their relationships and reputations.

Do Now:
Describe a time you solved a disagreement without it turning into a bigger issue.

_____
_____
_____
_____
_____
_____
_____
_____
_____

Mini-Lesson:
- Conflict is unavoidable; chaos is optional.
- A wise person can turn an enemy into an ally.

Activity:
Conflict Resolution Practice:
- Role-play conflict scenarios and brainstorm peaceful solutions.

Critical Thinking Questions:
1. Why is it important to master conflict resolution for leadership and peace?

_____
_____
_____
_____
_____
_____
_____
_____
_____
_____
_____
_____
_____
_____
_____

2. How does emotional maturity impact how you handle disagreements?

_____

_____

_____

_____

_____

_____

_____

_____

Journal Prompt:
What conflict resolution skill will you focus on improving this year?
[Write two full paragraphs.]

_____

_____

_____

_____

_____

_____

_____

_____

_____

_____

_____

_____

_____

_____

_____

_____

_____

_____

_____

_____

_____

_____

_____

Lesson 2: Group Cooperation

Objective:
Students will understand how to effectively collaborate with others toward shared goals.

Do Now:
Think about the best team you've ever been part of — what made it successful?

_____
_____
_____
_____
_____
_____
_____
_____
_____
_____

_Mini-Lesson:
- Cooperation is power — no dynasty was built alone.
- Teams win when every individual plays their role with excellence.

Activity:
Team Challenge:
- Small groups work together to solve a problem or complete a project.

Critical Thinking Questions:
1. Why is it important to trust and respect others when working as a team?

_____
_____
_____
_____
_____
_____
_____
_____
_____
_____
_____
_____
_____

2. How does teamwork prepare you for success in life and leadership?

_____

_____

_____

_____ —   —   _____

_____

_____

_____

_____

Journal Prompt:

What role do you usually take on in a group — leader, supporter, organizer? How can you strengthen that role?

[Write two full paragraphs.]

_____

_____

_____

_____

_____

_____

_____

_____

_____

_____

_____

_____

_____

_____

_____

_____

_____

_____

_____

_____

_____

Lesson 3: Friendship

Objective:
Students will reflect on the qualities of authentic friendships and learn to build stronger, healthier connections.

Do Now:
What is one quality you value most in a friend?

_____
_____
_____
_____
_____
_____
_____
_____
_____

Mini-Lesson:
- Friendship is chosen family.
- True friends grow you, not drain you.

Activity:
Friendship Reflection:
- List the top 5 qualities you want in a friend.
- Reflect on which qualities you bring to friendships.

Critical Thinking Questions:
1. How do friendships influence your self-esteem and future?

_____
_____
_____
_____
_____
_____
_____
_____
_____
_____
_____
_____
_____

2. Why is it important to choose friends based on values, not popularity?

_____

_____

_____

_____   _____

_____

_____

_____

_____

Journal Prompt:

What is one action you can take this week to strengthen or build a healthy friendship?
[Write two full paragraphs.]

_____

_____

_____

_____

_____

_____

_____

_____

_____

_____

_____

_____

_____

_____

_____

_____

_____

_____

_____

_____

_____

_____

Lesson 4: Identifying Unhealthy Relationships

Objective:
Students will learn how to recognize unhealthy or toxic relationships and create boundaries to protect their peace.

Do Now:
Think of a time when a relationship (friendship, family, or other) made you feel drained. What signs did you notice?

_____
_____
_____
_____
_____
_____
_____

Mini-Lesson:
- Protect your peace like it's priceless — because it is.
- Unhealthy relationships steal focus, energy, and growth.

Activity:
Relationship Health Check:
- List 5 signs of a healthy relationship.
- List 5 signs of an unhealthy or toxic relationship.

Critical Thinking Questions:
1. Why is it sometimes hard to walk away from unhealthy relationships?

_____
_____
_____
_____
_____
_____
_____
_____
_____
_____
_____
_____
_____
_____

2. How does protecting your energy set you up for success?

_____
_____
_____
_____
_____
_____
_____
_____

Journal Prompt:
What boundary are you ready to set to protect your peace?
[Write two full paragraphs.]

_____
_____
_____
_____
_____
_____
_____
_____
_____
_____
_____
_____
_____
_____
_____
_____
_____
_____
_____
_____
_____

Lesson 5: Self-Love

Objective:
Students will understand that self-love is the foundation for healthy relationships, success, and legacy.

Do Now:
What does self-love mean to you in one sentence?

_____
_____
_____
_____
_____
_____
_____
_____

Mini-Lesson:
- You teach the world how to treat you by how you treat yourself.
- Self-love isn't arrogance — it's alignment.

Activity:
Self-Love Contract:
- Write a contract to yourself stating how you will honor, protect, and uplift yourself daily.

Critical Thinking Questions:
1. How does self-love change the way you make decisions?

_____
_____
_____
_____
_____
_____
_____
_____
_____
_____
_____
_____
_____

2. Why is self-love a necessary act of revolution and survival?

_____
_____
_____
_____
_____
_____
_____
_____

Journal Prompt:
What promises will you keep to yourself starting today?
[Write two full paragraphs.]

_____
_____
_____
_____
_____
_____
_____
_____
_____
_____
_____
_____
_____
_____
_____
_____
_____
_____
_____
_____
_____
_____

Lesson 6: Communication Skills

Objective:
Students will develop the ability to express themselves clearly, listen actively, and connect effectively.

Do Now:
Think of a time when clear communication helped you succeed. What happened?

_____
_____
_____
_____
_____
_____
_____
_____
_____

Mini-Lesson:
- Your voice is a tool — sharpen it.
- Great communicators are powerful listeners too.

Activity:
Communication Power Practice:
- Practice active listening exercises and elevator pitches introducing yourself confidently.

Critical Thinking Questions:
1. How does good communication build trust and influence?

_____
_____
_____
_____
_____
_____
_____
_____
_____
_____
_____
_____
_____
_____

2. Why is listening often more powerful than speaking?

_____
_____
_____
_____
_____
_____
_____
_____

Journal Prompt:
What is one way you will practice stronger communication this week?
[Write two full paragraphs.]

_____
_____
_____
_____
_____
_____
_____
_____
_____
_____
_____
_____
_____
_____
_____
_____
_____
_____
_____
_____

Lesson 7: Emotional Intelligence

Objective:
Students will understand emotional intelligence and why managing emotions wisely leads to success and strong relationships.

Do Now:
Why do you think some people succeed despite challenges, while others collapse under pressure?

_____
_____
_____
_____
_____
_____
_____

Mini-Lesson:
- Emotional Intelligence (EQ) is knowing yourself, reading others, and choosing powerful responses.
- EQ > IQ when it comes to leadership and legacy.

Activity:
EQ Check:
- List 5 ways to manage emotions in stressful situations.

Critical Thinking Questions:
1. How does emotional intelligence separate leaders from followers?

_____
_____
_____
_____
_____
_____
_____
_____
_____
_____
_____
_____
_____
_____

2. Why is mastering your emotions a form of mastering your destiny?

_____
_____
_____
_____
_____
_____
_____
_____

Journal Prompt:
What emotional intelligence strategy will you apply starting today?
[Write two full paragraphs.]

_____
_____
_____
_____
_____
_____
_____
_____
_____
_____
_____
_____
_____
_____
_____
_____
_____
_____
_____
_____
_____
_____
_____
_____

Post-Reflection Survey

After completing the Knowledge of SELF curriculum, reflect on the following:

1. What is something new you learned about yourself?

2. How has your definition of success changed?

3. What parts of your identity do you embrace more now than before?

4. What are three personal goals you now feel ready to achieve?

5. How will you use what you've learned to uplift others?

TM

Knowledge
of S.E.L.F.
Curriculum

™

www.ingramcontent.com/pod-product-compliance
Lightning Source LLC
Chambersburg PA
CBHW052117020426
42335CB00021B/2804